The Role of

Emergency Care

as a Child Welfare Service

Emily Joyce Oakes and Madelyn Freundlich

CWLA Press
Washington, DC

The Child Welfare League of America is the nation's oldest and largest membership-based child welfare organization. We are committed to engaging people everywhere in promoting the well-being of children, youth, and their families, and protecting every child from harm.

CHILD WELFARE LEAGUE OF AMERICA, INC.
HEADQUARTERS
440 First Street NW, Third Floor
Washington, DC 20001-2085
E-mail: books@cwla.org

ISBN 13: 978-1-58760-027-2
ISBN 10: 1-58760-027-7

CURRENT PRINTING (last digit)

10 9 8 7 6 5 4 3 2 1

Printed in the United States of America

Cover and text layout by James D. Melvin

Edited by Julie Gwin

Library of Congress Cataloging-in-Publication Data

Oakes, Emily Joyce.

The role of emergency care as a child welfare service/Emily Joyce Oakes and Madelyn Freundlich.

p. cm.

Includes bibliographical references.

ISBN-13: 978-1-58760-027-2 (pbk. : alk. paper)

ISBN-10: 1-58760-027-7 (pbk. : alk. paper)

1. Child welfare--United States. 2. Foster children--Services for--United States. 3. Youth shelters--United States. 4. Foster home care--United States. I. Freundlich, Madelyn. II. Child Welfare League of America. III. Title.

HV741.O22 2005

362.73--dc22

2005013699

CWLA
gratefully acknowledges the
financial support of Children's Rights, Inc.,
which helped make this volume possible.

Contents

ACKNOWLEDGMENTS

The authors, both of whom are staff members at Children's Rights, acknowledge the support of the Annie E. Casey Foundation, whose generosity made this project possible. The authors express their appreciation to the valued members of the study's advisory board: Kathy Barbell, Senior Program Director for Program Operations, Child Welfare League of America, Washington, DC; Judith Goodhand, Senior Fellow, Annie E. Casey Foundation, Washington, DC; Elizabeth Leatherman, Technical Assistant, Annie E. Casey Foundation, Columbia, SC; and Jake Terpstra, Child Welfare Consultant, Grand Rapids, MI. The guidance, support, and insight of these child welfare professionals greatly enriched the research, analysis, and recommendations set forth in this study.

The authors also extend their appreciation to Courtney Abrams, Jana Bockstein, and Jessica Heldman, who reviewed drafts of this report and provided feedback that strengthened the presentation of the findings. Appreciation is also extended to Adira Siman for contributing her legal research expertise and to Carmen Hernandez for contributing her administrative expertise to the production of this report.

Introduction

When child welfare caseworkers take children into protective custody, they frequently rely on emergency care services for children's initial placements. These services are designed to be short-term, transitional arrangements for children's care while caseworkers make appropriate, stable, and, if needed, longer-term care arrangements. Although emergency care can take many different forms depending on the structure and practices of a state's or county's child welfare system, three major types exist: emergency shelters, emergency family foster care, and receiving centers. This report examines how agencies use these three forms of emergency care services independently or in conjunction with one another for children who must enter the foster care system and cannot be placed with kin caregivers. Through the use of case studies, the report describes selected communities' efforts to reduce or eliminate their reliance on emergency care to better serve children, youth, and families. The report concludes with a set of guiding principles and recommendations for communities that seek to make changes in their current systems of emergency care.

Chapter 1

The Current Knowledge Base on Emergency Care

Emergency shelter care, emergency family foster care, and receiving centers[1] are the principal types of emergency care services. The Child Welfare League of America (CWLA, 2004) defined emergency shelter care as a service designed to meet children's basic needs for safety, food, shelter, clothing, education, and recreation on a short-term basis that allows access and admission on a 24-hour basis. Barth (2002) wrote that *shelter care* is

> a term used to describe centralized emergency shelters that children [are] taken to by police or child welfare workers while decisions are made about...future placements. Typically, these planned stays may be for as short as one night and as long as 30 days—sometimes they last much longer. (p. 31)

Barth (2002) described *emergency family foster care* as

> a foster home that is especially designed and funded to care for... children for a few days, weeks, or months. [These] homes routinely care for smaller children but may be used for adolescents. Providers are typically given a per diem rate per bed, whether or not the bed has a child in it—this assures that a space will be available when needed. (p. 31)

CWLA (1995) defined family foster care as a planned service in which the temporary protection and nurturing of children takes place in the homes of licensed foster families, but it does not specifically define emergency family foster care.

3

Receiving centers are a new phenomenon, and the services they provide are described differently in different geographical regions of the United States. No consensus definition currently exists for receiving centers. CWLA, for example, does not reference receiving centers in its standards, although CWLA standards do describe short-term or diagnostic services, which typically are provided by receiving centers. Barth (2002) described receiving centers as a "child-friendly, temporary environment in which children who have been removed from their homes can wait, be fed, sleep, [and] be comforted...prior to going to their next setting" (p. 31). This report defines receiving centers as very short-term programs designed to provide assessment, crisis intervention, stabilization, and placement or other postdischarge planning.

The research literature on emergency shelter care, emergency family foster care, and receiving centers is not extensive. The following discussion, however, summarizes the current knowledge regarding these three forms of emergency care.

Emergency Shelter Care as a Placement Resource

Emergency shelter care is used in many communities throughout the United States as the initial placement for children and youth when they enter foster care. In many communities, shelters are the principal response to the placement needs of children on entry into care. In theory, shelters are designed to provide temporary care for children while caseworkers attempt to locate other longer-term, stable arrangements with kin or foster families, or, if necessary, in group homes or residential treatment centers. In practice, however, children often remain in shelters for months. The effect on children of extended stays in a "temporary" placement is compounded by other realities of shelter care. Children living in shelters often are not enrolled in school, do not receive appropriate medical care or mental health services, and do not have the support of consistent caregivers who can assist them with the emotional effects of separation from their parents and their entry into foster care. For these reasons, some communities have reevaluated their use of emergency shelters as a placement resource for children and have developed alternative responses to children's needs for care.

The research literature has given very limited attention to emergency shelter care and includes very little in the form of critical assessment. In the 1960s and 1970s, emergency shelter care for children was a standard service response to the placement needs of youth entering foster care (American Association of University Women, 1970). It was not until the mid-1980s that Jake Terpstra (1988) of the U.S. Children's Bureau wrote one of the first analytic papers, published by CWLA, on the role of emergency shelters. This paper raised a number of issues about the advantages and disadvantages of group shelter care compared with family-based care and outlined the "essential program components" that shelter care should incorporate to meet children's needs. Since Terpstra's work, however, researchers have performed little critical assessment of the use of emergency shelter care. Agencies have continued to use shelters without research that documents the effectiveness of the service or careful assessments of the effect of shelter care on children and youth.

To the extent that the literature addresses emergency shelter care, the focus typically has been on pragmatic considerations. Johnson (2003), for example, suggested that the "current shortage of alternative placement options often makes emergency shelters a necessary interim step in the placement process for many children and youth" (p. 6). Other commentators note that emergency shelter care is widely used because it is a readily available placement option. Some observers have stated that in many communities, shelters are the entry point into the foster care system for many, if not all, children and youth (Litronik, Taussig, Landsverk, & Garland, 1999; Rittner,

1995). Others report that some communities also use shelters as a last resort for children for whom all other types of placements have been exhausted (Litronik et al., 1999).

The extent to which emergency shelters are used in most communities, however, is not clear. The U.S. Department of Health and Human Services (DHHS) does not track the use of emergency shelters as placement resources for children and youth in its Adoption and Foster Care Analysis and Reporting System (AFCARS), and such data are consequently available only if states or counties choose voluntarily to track this information. Data from California, for example, are available, and data covering a one-year period (April 1, 2003, to March 31, 2004) indicate that of the 27,295 children who entered foster care for the first time in that state, almost one-fifth (4,845) went immediately into a group home or shelter (Needell et al., 2004).

Barth (2002), in an examination of the use of institutional care and family-centered care, found that the placement of children in group care settings is often justified on the basis that their behavior cannot be managed in family foster care or kinship care and their needs require a highly structured environment. Nonetheless, he found that the outcomes for children and youth placed in group care settings were not positive. Youth often had quite negative perceptions of group care, as did child welfare workers who often place children and adolescents in these facilities; the youth had fewer interpersonal relationships that supported their well-being; and they did not see shelters as safe or family-like (Barth, 2002). Specifically with regard to emergency shelters and their effect on children and youth, Barth (2002) observed that "centralized emergency shelters are not a necessary or efficient way to bring children into out-of-home care" (p. ii).

Some advocates and researchers, however, have promoted the use of group care and emergency shelters as therapeutic environments for children. Johnson (2003), for example, wrote that "positive structured programming allows emergency shelters to enrich the lives of the children they serve" (p. 7). Advocates of emergency shelters also state that they stabilize the emotional and behavioral status of children who enter out-of-home care. They highlight the ability of shelter staff to address a child's negative feelings, which may be exacerbated by the child's removal from their home; provide brief treatment for the child; and set a positive tone for parent interactions with the child (Gershowitz & MacFarlane, 1990; Johnson, 2003).

Some proponents maintain that shelters can decrease the number of moves that children must make while they are in foster care, but research suggests otherwise. In one study of children placed in shelters in a large metropolitan area of southeastern Florida, Rittner (1995) found that a majority of Hispanic and African American children entering care, most of whom were younger than 6 years of age, were initially placed in shelters. One-third (32%) of the children in the study experienced placement changes within their first six months in care.

A number of professionals have raised questions about the appropriateness of emergency shelter care when children must enter foster care. Terpstra (2003) described most emergency group care as a short-sighted solution to the shortage of foster families and emphasized that shelter care should never be necessary in small communities. Similarly, Barth (2002) and Kools (1997) maintained that shelters not only do not provide family-like environments, but in some cases, they do not keep children safe. They highlighted the dangers posed by placing large numbers of children of different ages into care together—children who exhibit different, and in some cases, serious, problems. Of particular concern is "contagious exposure to the problem behavior of older children" (Barth, 2002). Of concern to many observers is the high staff turnover rate as well as high turnover of residents, which may give staff little time to get to know the children, complicate treatment planning, and inhibit the development of relationships between children and staff (Gershowitz & MacFarlane, 1990; Johnson, 2003).

Family Foster Care and Receiving Centers as Placement Resources for Children and Youth

An alternative to placing children and adolescents in emergency shelter care is placement with foster families who provide "emergency" care. Children placed with an emergency foster family are placed with foster parents who are responsible for their care on a time-limited basis (24 hours to several months, depending on the state and county), until they are either reunited with their families or placed in a longer-term foster care arrangement. In many cases, children placed with foster families on an emergency basis remain with them if continuing foster care is needed and the foster family is willing to care for the child on a longer-term basis.

In some areas of the country, children's placements with foster families are facilitated through the use of receiving centers. Receiving centers provide care on a time-limited basis of usually less than 24 hours immediately on the children's removal from their parents' custody. Receiving centers provide brief assessments and a setting in which children can wait while a caseworker finds a foster family or kin caregiver for them.

Both of these forms of emergency care have been promoted as more beneficial for children and youth than shelter care. Although primarily promoted for infants and young children, some have viewed emergency family foster care as a standard for all children because it is less traumatizing for children and youth and meets their developmental and emotional needs, particularly as they experience the disruption and trauma of removal from their birthfamilies (Barth, 2002; Choice, Deichert, Legry, & Austin, 2000; DeSena et al., 2003; Terpstra,

2003). Researchers have also promoted receiving centers as encouraging permanence by providing an immediate assessment of the child and information to support placement decisions so that the first placement is the child's last placement (Choice et al., 2000*)*.

Emergency Family Foster Care

The research literature provides little information on the use or effectiveness of emergency family foster care. McDonald, Allen, Westerfelt and Piliavin (1996) examined outcomes associated with family foster care and group care in general and concluded that children who are placed and remain with foster families tended to function better as adults than children who spent at least some of their time in residential care. The researchers, however, observed that poorer outcomes may be related to emotional, physical, and mental difficulties that lead to the need for group care. Other studies (Festinger, 1983; Jones & Moses, 1984) have suggested that children placed in family foster care have more positive outcomes than children in group care, including: attainment of higher levels of education, the likelihood of having close friends, stronger informal support networks, and more positive assessments of their lives.

The literature documents that group care costs are 2 to 10 times higher than the cost of family foster care and treatment foster care (Barth, 2002; DeSena et al., 2003; Terpstra, 2003). One California county, for example, reported that it spent $8,370 for a child's stay of one month at a shelter compared with about $800 for a month of care by a foster family (De Sá, 2003). In their evaluation of the SAFE Homes program, a group care program used in Connecticut, DeSena and colleagues (2003) concluded that

> expenditures associated with placement of children in group care settings are prohibitive. Rather than use the available limited resources to house children in a group setting, at the time of first removal, children should be placed in traditional foster care placements and provided supplemental assessment and case management services. (p. 17)

Receiving Centers

As a new child welfare service, receiving centers have received little attention in the literature. Choice et al. (2000) conducted an exploratory study of receiving center programs in Contra Costa County, California. They described these centers as designed to receive children immediately on their removal from their parents' custody and facilitate the child's transition into foster care. They typically do not house children, but instead, meet children's immediate needs by providing a comfortable place to stay, a shower, snacks, and a clean change of clothes while caseworkers find temporary or longer-term care arrangements. Receiving centers also provide brief, informal assessments of children to gain a better understanding of the child's needs (Choice et al., 2000). With the goal of making the first placement the only and last placement for children entering care, receiving centers give caseworkers a limited amount of time (24 hours or less) to explore possible care with kin or with a foster family who can meet children's longer-term needs, as opposed to placing a child with any foster family that is available at the time children come into care.

In their study of the receiving center program in Contra Costa County, Choice and colleagues (2000) found that prior to the county's development of the receiving centers, caseworkers often located placements while transporting children in their cars or while children waited in their offices. Case record reviews and focus groups revealed that children who were served through the receiving centers were more likely to have relatives involved in their cases, receive more services, and reunify with families than children who were not (Choice et al., 2000). Receiving center staff and social workers cited as the benefits of receiving centers their convenience, their safety, and the role they played in detraumatizing children's experiences. These professionals believed that receiving centers helped social workers make more thoughtful placements for children.

On the other hand, however, the researchers found that children served through receiving centers were more likely to experience more out-of-home placements and have their cases open six months after entry into care (Choice et al., 2000). The researchers also found that foster parents did not always have positive views of receiving centers. Foster parents expressed concern that receiving centers simply added to the trauma of the children's removal as they "move from one scary situation to another" (Choice et al., 2000, p. 42). Many foster parents stated they were not informed about the purpose of receiving centers or the services provided and believed that centers provided services "variably and insufficiently" (Choice et al., 2000). Foster parents, however, commented that children were sometimes "less stressed" after spending time at a receiving center (Choice et al., 2000).

In his analysis, Barth (2002) recommended using receiving centers combined with emergency family foster care or small group homes as an alternative to emergency shelters. He suggested that using receiving centers may improve retention of emergency foster parents because children are likely to be calmer when they are placed with foster parents; the child can be placed with the family at a time that is more convenient to the foster parent, as opposed to in the middle of the night; and center staff can provide foster parents with more complete information about the child (Barth, 2002). Nonetheless, he cautioned that because of the extremely limited period of time that children may remain at receiving centers, they may not be very effective in helping children who have experienced significant problems in foster care, such as children who have experienced multiple placements.

CHAPTER 2

The Method

In an effort to better understand the use of emergency shelter care, emergency family foster care, and receiving centers, Children's Rights conducted a qualitative study involving interviews with child welfare professionals and case studies of selected communities that have attempted to redesign their emergency care programs. Through interviews with child welfare professionals, researchers gathered information about current emergency care practice. They conducted interviews with a convenience sample of 16 child welfare researchers and child welfare administrators (referred to here as key informants) from across the United States. The key informants represented nine states[1] and the District of Columbia. They were identified by the project's National Advisory Board[2] and the project researchers and were further developed through a sampling technique known as snowball sampling.[3] The researchers selected the key informants based on their knowledge of emergency care practice in general or in a specific geographic area. Researchers interviewed the key informants by telephone using a standardized interview protocol. The researchers, consultants, county administrators, and leaders of community agencies who were interviewed provided insights into current emergency care practice in states and counties across the United States. Chapter 3, "Current Emergency

Care Practice," presents the findings from the key informant interviews.

Chapter 4, "Changes in Emergency Care Practice: Three Case Studies," provides the results of an examination of efforts in three communities to improve practices related to the placement of children and youth when they enter foster care. The researchers and the study's National Advisory Board selected the case study sites after extensive research and discussion regarding various communities' efforts to address emergency care issues. The researchers conducted interviews with individual county administrators and program managers for each selected site. The interviews were designed to gain a comprehensive picture of the community's child welfare system, the emergency care services that it offers, and an assessment from the perspectives of the county administrators and program managers of the community's efforts to improve emergency care practice. The researchers also used academic databases and the Internet to obtain supplemental information about the selected communities.

CHAPTER 3

Current Emergency Care Practice

Emergency care services are intended to offer temporary care for children and youth entering the foster care system while caseworkers make decisions about the appropriate next steps for children and their families. Increasingly, however, concerns have been expressed that emergency care too often becomes longer-term care for children because workers do not make other care arrangements. Although many states and counties have written policies that place limits on the time that children may remain in emergency care, they often serve merely as guidelines, and in some cases, they are so poorly defined that caseworkers are unclear about the limitations on their use. At the same time, concerns have grown about the effect of emergency services on children and youth. As well-being has become an outcome of greater focus, child welfare professionals have given attention to the potential negative effects of emergency care on children's physical, emotional, and developmental status. The following describes the results of interviews with 16 key informants, which focused on current practice with regard to emergency shelters, emergency family foster homes, and receiving centers and outcomes associated with their use.

Emergency Shelter Care for Children and Youth Entering the Foster Care System

Current child welfare practice standards reflect an acceptance of emergency shelter care as a placement option when children and youth enter foster care. CWLA standards, for example, acknowledge emergency shelter care as a child welfare service. In its *Standards of Excellence for Services for Abused and Neglected Children and Their Families,* CWLA (1999) stated that "child protection agencies should have immediate access to emergency shelter services for children," although it counsels that "infants, toddlers, and other particularly vulnerable children" should be placed "in a family setting or other resource able to meet their need for nurturance and attention" (Standard 1.28). Similarly, CWLA's *Standards of Excellence for Residential Services* (2004) recognize emergency shelter care programs of less than 24 hours to a maximum of 45 days as an essential component in the array of residential service settings (Standards 1.1, 1.7).

The child welfare professionals who were interviewed in this study reported different experiences with emergency shelters. Some key informants reported that child welfare systems rely very heavily on emergency shelters, whereas other respondents reported that some counties have banned emergency shelter care altogether. Shelter care, for example, is "vital" to Arizona's system, with every district in Arizona having a shelter; Rhode Island relies heavily on shelters, but they are small and serve four to eight residents in home-like environments. In Iowa, as the result of a funding shortfall that forced the state to cap the number of children and youth who are placed in residential treatment, caseworkers place children in "holding patterns" in emergency shelters until they can be placed in residential treatment centers. In Lucas County, Ohio, emergency shelters have been eliminated, and workers place children with foster families on their entry into foster care.

A majority of key informants believed that emergency shelter care is used more extensively in urban areas and large counties. One interviewee stated:

> [Areas with] less density, meaning not overwhelming numbers of cases, perhaps have better practice, because there isn't the economic incentive to build a shelter. One of the biggest indicators of whether a child will end up in a facility is the proximity of the facility itself. In more sparsely populated areas, they don't have the numbers [of children in care] to justify having a shelter. [I believe these are the areas] where you'll find better practice. [Shelters are] a function of the [caseload] density. Shelter use is also a matter of convenience [for the caseworker or the police]. If it's more convenient to put a kid in a shelter, they go to a shelter. If it's not convenient, then they don't [go to the shelter] except in, maybe, very special cases.

Another respondent attributed differences between rural and urban areas to the structure of child welfare systems:

> A main difference between rural and urban shelters is the increased volume of children in urban areas and the number of staff needed to serve these children. [Our state] tries to centralize entry into foster care in urban areas so [shelters] don't exceed licensing capacity. For rural areas, workers usually go through a licensing agency for placement of children because there is not nearly the same volume of kids coming into care, and a large centralized shelter doesn't make sense. In rural areas, there's a much more formal structure for placement and access [to] emergency foster homes than there is access to emergency shelters. Providers in urban areas don't use foster homes nearly as much as they use shelters or other residential placements because foster homes are a scarce resource.

Key informants stated that children placed in emergency shelters tend to be older (12 to 17 years old), to be members of minority ethnic groups (with a disproportionate number of African American children in shelters), and to have significant physical or mental health problems. These observations are consistent with research that has described the age, race or ethnicity, and health characteristics of children who generally are placed in residential care (Barth, 2002; Ensign, 2001; Litrownik et al., 1999).

Key informants offered a number of reasons children may be placed in shelters. Some foster families may wish to care only for young children or may not believe that they are able to care for a child with severe emotional or mental health problems. Several key informants noted that children whose family foster care arrangements have disrupted multiple times may need residential treatment, but because residential care may not be readily available, they may have no placement option other than shelter care. Caseworkers may also see shelter care as the only option for large sibling groups if the goal is to keep siblings together.

Key informants commented that the time children spend in shelter care is related to a number of factors:

- a child's individual circumstances and needs;
- the age of the child—older children remain in shelter care longer;
- the race or ethnicity of a child—African American children remain in shelter care longer;
- whether a child has behavioral, emotional, or substance abuse problems—children with more problems tend to remain in shelter care longer;
- the degree of a child's developmental difficulties;
- whether the child is part of a large sibling group;
- the availability of foster family homes as placement resources—if shelters are convenient, caseworkers and police are more likely to place children in shelters; and
- the caseloads of child protective service workers—larger caseloads result in less individual attention to each child,

with a greater likelihood that a caseworker will rely on shelter care.

Longer stays in shelter care also are associated with insufficient efforts to plan adequately for a child's next placement. One key informant stated:

> The way of thinking about things is not to say you have 20 days in this shelter bed. What happens is, instead of [caseworkers] working on the kid's discharge plan from the minute they walk in the door, they wait until the 19th day and then they start thinking that they need to move this kid [because of prescribed time limits], and then the kid has no place to go. So there's no one moving the case forward and paying attention to it [on a daily basis].

States and counties have established time limits on children's stays in emergency shelter care, but based on information from key informants and current data, limits alone are not effective in ensuring that children and youth are placed in a timely way in a longer-term care arrangement. In California, the law limits shelter care stays to 90 days (California Health and Safety Code, Section 1502.3, 2004), and the mean length of stay for children in shelters is 30 days (Needell et al., 2004). Nonetheless, some children remain in shelters for many months and even years waiting to be moved to a more permanent arrangement. In Arizona, which does not specify a time limit on children's stays in shelter care, children and youth remain in shelter care for an average of 81 days, according to a key informant. Connecticut's policy dictates that children remain in shelter care for no longer than 30 days, with one 15-day extension available to caseworkers if needed. A key informant from Connecticut, however, reported that statewide, the average length of shelter stays for children and youth is 71 days.

There was general agreement among key informants that shelter care can make children's transition into out-of-home care more diffi-

cult. They described the negative effects of shelter care on children as
follows:

> Every time they move in and out of the shelter, it's another
> placement. For [caseworkers] who are often overwhelmed,
> it's convenient for them to park a kid in a shelter. This
> means that working for permanency, or holding the foster
> family together, or having programs that support kids in
> placements aren't thought about because the shelters are
> there and you can put a kid in shelter. You don't have to
> work to find additional services.

> It's hard enough for kids to adjust to one or two or three or
> four members of a foster family, and kids are often stymied
> by that. To try to deal with all the different people in a con-
> gregate care setting is really overwhelming for children.
> Especially if the child is in congregate care that lasts more
> than a very short time—like a day or so.

> When we put kids in shelter care, we send the message that
> they did something wrong. That they're going into an insti-
> tution of sorts, with the changing staff and all these other
> kids, and the message is that they did something wrong,
> which is why they were taken from their family and put in
> this place instead of being put with another family.

Some key informants commented on the limited services in shelters and the challenges of managing care for children with a variety of
needs:

> Basically we have kids in a shelter setting where they're not
> getting treatment. Therefore, at best, they're maintaining
> their condition and more likely, their condition is probably
> deteriorating. So, in the end, if they do get the treatment, if
> they ever do, they need to make up for the fact that they've
> deteriorated since they first came into care. Couple this issue
> with kids who are in shelter for "regular" shelter care needs,
> and you have kids living in situations with other very trou-
> bled kids. This raises many safety and risk management con-
> cerns and, quite frankly, it creates a scarier situation for "reg-

ular" shelter kids and presents them with more stress. This is hard for staff to manage and for kids to manage. We want to keep kids safe and also keep them from beginning to develop or accumulate problems because they're in programs with other difficult kids.

The biggest issue heard from the shelter providers is that they take kids [with a variety of] needs. In contrast to residential care centers, which can focus on a specific population, such as girls with substance abuse problems, shelters don't have that luxury and have to take all kinds of kids and then meet the needs for those kids, and that's challenging. Even though the shelters have age ranges and can be divided by gender, the diversity of the children and their problems is very difficult.

Another key informant emphasized that the individual needs of children are not well met in shelter care:

In group care, you have to make rules for the group and focus on group dynamics, not the exact needs of each child. In group care, rules are always made for the majority of the group. Kids who act out get all the attention, and kids who are quiet get nothing. For this reason, quiet kids don't get what they need. [Family] foster care allows people to look at what's really happening with a kid, individually.

Several key informants stated that shelters typically provide a minimum level of services. They noted that shelters are not designed to provide treatment but, instead, to provide basic care for children. Because shelter care is intended to be temporary, most shelters do not work with children and families on an ongoing basis. They may provide initial assessments of children, but even in this area of service, shelters are not equipped to address the serious behavioral and emotional problems that children entering foster care now often present.

Some key informants expressed particular concerns about children's education while they are in shelter care. One respondent stated:

> [The Department of Children and Families (DCF)] doesn't
> advocate for children to stay in their own schools when they
> enter care. There's a lot of confusion about the laws among
> caseworkers. DCF doesn't have any policy recognizing that
> children are entitled to the protections of the McKinney-
> Vento Act [the federal law that entitles homeless children to
> educational services]. Some shelters have schools in the shel-
> ter—which is illegal. We need to solve the problem of kids
> sitting around three to four weeks waiting to get put into
> school once they're in the shelter.

Other key informants, however, stated that shelters in their communities make efforts to ensure that children attend their schools of
origin.

When discussing the quality of shelter care, key informants consistently focused on the staffing of shelters and the physical safety of
children in these facilities. With regard to emergency shelter staff, one
key informant stated:

> There are some kids who report being treated like they're in
> juvenile detention and, based on their stories, I think the
> staff [are] antagonistic towards the kids. There are other sto-
> ries I hear from kids who say the staff try to make the expe-
> rience good for kids.

Key informants also commented on the difficulties that staff
encounter in developing and sustaining a quality shelter environment:

> You never have the same group of kids, the same time of the
> day, two days in a row. It's very hard to monitor what chil-
> dren are going to be put together in a shelter setting. I've seen
> some shelters that provide good care. The indicators to me
> are smaller rather than larger. But its very difficult given the
> transitory nature of shelters, the mixed populations of kids,
> and the complex needs of the children using shelter care.

> We tend to think of [shelters] as large, bureaucratic, and
> institutional with run-down facilities, and that isn't neces-
> sarily the case. Some are more welcoming and more atten-
> tive to the developmental needs of kids, but it's very hard for

shelters to maintain that standard of care for very long because when no one has particular responsibility for something, it doesn't get done. When everyone has responsibility for kids, nobody has responsibility for them to a certain extent. I think if you give that responsibility to a family, they're going to fulfill it and fulfill it better, although we've had many failures with foster families as well. I think it's a structural issue, when you have shifts of people who are caring for kids, who are coming and going, it's very hard to make a connection and keep that connection with the children.

Key informants reported the safety of children in shelters to be highly variable among facilities. They reported that the risk of abuse and neglect was greater in emergency shelters than in family foster care, that older children often abuse younger children when children of different ages are placed together, and that there are particular dangers when juvenile offenders are placed with dependent children in foster care. One key informant stated: "You can't make a shelter like a home environment and provide the types of protections parents provide."

Almost universally, key informants highlighted the negative effects of congregate care. One respondent urged that congregate care settings not be used for children:

I think we should be making every effort to abolish the use of congregate care for children when they enter into care. Children need families. Children have a developmental timeline that is different from ours—nothing is short-term to a child. A day or a couple of days is very important to a child. We take that much too lightly as adults. We think like adults, not like children.

Others recommended that if communities must use shelters, they should create smaller facilities (from four to eight beds) to better provide a safe and home-like environment for children who enter foster care.

Family Foster Care and Receiving Centers for Children and Youth Entering the Foster Care System

As noted earlier, CWLA's *Standards of Excellence for Family Foster Care Services* (1995) do not specifically define emergency family foster care, and instead, define family foster care as

> an essential child welfare service for children and their parents who must live apart from each other for a temporary period of time... family foster care should respond to the needs of children and... be based on premises that emphasize the safety and well-being of the child. (Standards 1.2, 1.3)

Similarly, as noted previously, there are no standards concerning receiving centers. CWLA's *Standards of Excellence for Residential Services* (2004), however, refer to "short-term/diagnostic services," which appear to mirror some of the services that receiving centers offer. These services include "short-term assessment, intensive family assessment, and immediate attention to a child's crisis situation, including: crisis intervention, stabilization, diagnostic assessment, and placement or other post-discharge planning" (Standard 1.8). What differentiates the services provided by receiving centers is the duration of time that these services are provided—typically no longer than 24 hours.

The researchers asked key informants about both emergency family foster care and receiving centers. They viewed emergency foster family homes as the best type of emergency care service. Many believed that emergency foster parents can be successful in stabilizing children when they enter care and can readily obtain the assessments and services that children need. One key informant compared emergency family foster care to other types of care:

> Some people don't want emergency family foster care because they want the first placement to be the last place-

ment. I want the first placement to be the last placement, and I want to push permanency too, but I see emergency family foster care as a lesser of two evils. I'd rather have specially trained, available, emergency family foster homes to take kids instead of putting them in shelters. Ultimately, would I rather see the kid matched perfectly with the ideal foster family in their community that's totally appropriate for this kid? Absolutely. It's a real conundrum. I don't think you want to have emergency family foster care so the emergency foster placement is three days, pack your bag, and get out of here, but if it's done thoughtfully with lots of support, it's a good option.

Respondents reported that communities' use of emergency family foster care varies significantly. Some states, such as Ohio and Rhode Island, use emergency family foster care extensively, but in most states, including these states, the supply of foster families is limited. Some key informants reported that agencies typically use emergency foster families only for children who have special needs, such as medically fragile children, because emergency shelters and group homes cannot provide the structure and care that these children need. One emergency foster family program that was highlighted was the Host Homes program, operated by an organization called Connecting Point in Lucas County, Ohio. The Host Homes program provides therapeutic foster care for children and youth through the age of 21. A key informant involved with this program stated:

> We're privileged to play a role in a kid's life and we're not here to replace the family. "Hosting" is a more friendly term that explains what we're trying to do. Hosting is a less permanent feeling. Our objective is not to replace the biological family but, instead, our objective is to be a host for children while we're working with them and their family to try to create permanency.

Although key informants agreed that emergency family foster care can be designed to serve all children, many clarified that it may not be appropriate for children who need more structured settings, including children who chronically run away and children with destructive behaviors. One respondent stated:

> For some kids, family foster care is not the right place. Some kids have been so traumatized that they simply can't do a close family setting. Given that, it doesn't mean they can't be in group care. Some kids need the anonymity of group care—when they're not the focus.

Another key informant explained:

> If [foster] care is needed, and we try to avoid it, then the preference for placement would be family foster care in every case. There are some risks associated [in family foster care] with older kids or kids who have significant mental illness. [There can be] significant violence that's involved, where clearly there's more risk or if you have kids with a long runaway history. There's a lot of risk with these [high-risk kids] being put in family foster care, so you need to be really careful [about placing them].

Key informants reported that age and race affect the type of emergency placements that caseworkers use for children. They agreed that younger children are easier to place with emergency foster families. Foster families often prefer to care for young children, and caseworkers are more likely to seek family placements for young children because of concerns about their developmental needs. Some key informants stated that white children are more likely to be placed in emergency family foster care than are nonwhite children. One key informant stated:

> Minority and poor kids wind up in congregate care more frequently than white, middle-class kids with the same problems. I'm not saying people are consciously prejudiced, but that people are systemically prejudiced. Systems tend to use what's available to them. Workers are going to use what they have.

Key informants also mentioned other factors that may affect the placement of children in emergency family foster care: the availability of emergency foster families in a community, the child's placement history with foster families, whether a child's prior placements have disrupted, and the child's behavior. Geography, as previously noted, also is a factor: Children in rural communities are more likely to be placed with foster families because the community has no shelters or other group care alternatives.

Key informants noted that many states and counties have time limits regarding children's stays in emergency family foster care. The time frame ranges from 2 or 3 days to 10 days or more. In some communities, fiscal considerations limit children's care with emergency foster families because these foster families receive a higher pay rate than regular foster families. Key informants, however, reported that although the intention is to maintain children with emergency foster families for a short period of time, other placement alternatives may not be available, and children may stay in their emergency care placements for longer than the prescribed limits. Emergency foster family stays also may be longer than intended because needed resources, particularly health and mental health services, cannot be obtained or because of court delays. Key informants further noted that emergency foster families often become permanent foster families because they grow attached to the child in their care. They saw this development both as a positive and a negative. On the positive side, children find permanence with these families, and on the negative side, a new emergency foster family must be found to replace the family that is no longer available. One key informant stated:

> Every placement is disruptive, so you don't want to move kids if you don't have to. So much of foster care placement is an "art" to get the right match between the provider and the child. When the match is really good, sometimes you just have to go with it.

Key informants described several advantages to emergency family foster care:

- it provides a more intimate and natural environment for children and youth,
- children are more likely to feel that they are receiving individualized attention in a family setting,
- the needs of each child are more likely to be met because the responsibility for the child's care rests with a parent,
- the first placement is more likely to be the last placement for the child, and
- it is more economical than group-based emergency care.

Many key informants also stated that children are safer with a family than they are in a congregate care setting. One respondent, for example, stated:

> For the child, it's pretty scary to be in an aggregate care setting when you don't know the other kids. [The caseworker doesn't] know the dynamics you are exposing a child to that come from an aggregate care setting. It's a lot harder to manage the different needs of the kids when you have [multiple] kids as opposed to one kid...It's a scary thing to expose them to one another and [you want to] make sure you keep everyone safe and aren't contributing to problems.

Key informants emphasized the constant battle to develop and sustain an adequate supply of quality emergency foster families. One key informant stated:

> No one really puts the effort into recruiting families. You really need to know what you're selling. We're still going after the emotional heartstrings recruitment approach, and what we need to be doing is recruiting for the job and looking at what people really like and want to do. We need to stop lying to people, and foster families need to know these kids have problems up front, and they need to be provided with supports to help themselves and to help that child.

One respondent described her community's recruitment and retention strategy for emergency foster parents:

> Relationship building is very important in retaining families. We also have a foster parent association that supports families in the system. They help us recruit and retain as well as run a mentoring program for new families for up to one year. We have a foster family dinner for them every year. We're also doing community-based recruitment and retention, and we're interviewing foster parents to see how we can do it better. We also have a 24-hour support hotline to support foster parents. We're also trying to develop a clinical hotline, as a resource for foster families.

Key informants, however, pointed to the lack of resources to develop emergency foster care programs and recruit and support families.

Key informants also identified other impediments to the use of emergency family foster care. One respondent stated, "Even though residential care is more expensive, it's easier to do than family foster care. It's easier to find a bed and stick a kid in it." Uncertainty about the child's needs also may make it difficult to place a child with a family, because it is harder to determine the best family options for the child if his or her needs are unclear. Key informants stated:

> When kids are coming into care, it's hard to determine what kids are really going to need from a service and support perspective, therefore making emergency foster care placements dangerous, because you don't know the child well or the dynamics of what you're dealing with a lot of times—which can be pretty scary.

> An advantage to shelter care is when kids are behaviorally out of control. We have professional staff at shelters who know how to deal with these kids, who have seen these behaviors before—we have a place to put these kids. Kids come to shelters who've had multiple disruptions in foster care [and] seem to settle better in the shelters. It's better than setting them up for another disruption in a foster home. We do need high-end foster homes for these kids, but it's hard

because foster parents usually have other children at home, and it's not good to place acting-out kids with families because they'll create a major disruption in the home and it's not good for younger children in the home [to be exposed to that].

Caseworkers may not be able to match a child and a foster family appropriately, particularly if the child is placed after usual work hours. In this connection, however, many key informants stated that kin often are the best resources for children and should be identified early, possibly averting the need to bring the child into foster care. One respondent spoke to the need to avoid foster care placements altogether:

Placement in general is tricky. I'm not as militant as saying [that placing high-risk children with foster families] should never happen, but I'm pretty cautious about it, and the system is often well intended but not necessarily helping with [its] solutions. I think placement is seen as being a solution sometimes, and it isn't.

Less than half of the key informants had information about the use of receiving centers for children entering foster care. The key informants who had knowledge of receiving centers were not able to draw conclusions about their effect on children, families, or child welfare practice. Their comments, however, provided an understanding of some of the potential benefits and drawbacks of receiving centers.

When asked to describe receiving centers, one respondent, who was quite knowledgeable about this service, provided a very positive picture of the role of receiving centers:

The receiving center idea is different—it's a facility, but the function of the facility is to receive children temporarily until they are placed in a foster home. It's time limited and the basic concept is that if a child is taken into custody, the child will be taken to a center. There are staff who look after children while social workers try to find a placement for the children in a private room so children don't have to listen to the social workers trying to find beds for them and feeling unwanted, scared, or listening to the social workers talk about them to the potential foster families. Children get food, a place to sleep, and some entertainment. On that shift, they move the kids into a foster home. If they can't move the kids in 23 hours, then they have to rely on a back-up like a residential care facility for the child's placement. Receiving centers are not licensed to provide shelter for children, which keeps them temporary.

This key informant highlighted the fact that receiving centers are open 24 hours a day and provide basic assessments of children that can take place at any time, thereby allowing caseworkers to make informed decisions about returning the child home, placing the child with kin, or placing the child with a foster family or in another setting. Other key informants agreed that services provided by receiving centers support good placement decisions:

[The receiving centers] can prevent placement failures because they're a means to provide a thorough assessment of the child and make sure they are appropriately placed. This prevents kids from "failing into a placement."

[The receiving center] is our attempt at increasing our odds [for finding the right placement] and not screwing up. If we're not sure on information or on the needs of the child, and we need to take a day or two to figure it out to make sure we have a decent match, we'll access [the assistance center] and try to avoid the need for foster placement at all.

Some key informants, however, were quite critical of receiving centers. One stated:

[Receiving centers] measure the kid in an artificial setting and [it is important to recognize] that all kids don't need the "Cadillac assessment." These assessments become standardized very quickly and become almost meaningless—not individualized. I'd rather have professional assessors on staff who can address children's need in an individual way and work with a treatment team, rather than have a clinician who can diagnose problems. [For children] where there may be very special needs, I'm not against residential assessment. But I don't want it to be justified as a first congregate care stop for all kids based on [the need to] assess.

Similarly, another key informant disputed the capacity of receiving centers to provide assessments and focused on the role that families play in obtaining needed assessments for children:

The notion for [receiving] centers is to give the child a comfortable place to wait while the worker tries to find an immediate home for the child that night. I think it's window dressing to pretend it's anything else. Of course children and families need to be assessed, but they can be assessed in a home. It's not about the placement match. I think that's way overblown. You recruit good, solid, strong families that understand there's a need for them to parent children, and you do some basic checks of information that you have readily available, and you put that kid in a home. The rest of the assessment, that you very much need to do, you do after the child is with a family. The family can bring them somewhere and you then do the assessment of the child, the birthfamily, and their needs.

Chapter 4

Changes in Emergency Care Practice: Three Case Studies

This section discusses findings from case studies of three county-administered child welfare systems that have developed new approaches to meeting the placement needs of children entering foster care: El Paso County, Colorado; Marion County, Indiana; and Contra Costa County, California. Each case study presents the community's philosophy about the use of emergency care services and highlights the practice, social, and political factors that have shaped the community's response to the placement needs of children entering foster care. The case studies focus on the processes that each community used to change its emergency care practices, as well as the factors that facilitated or hindered its change efforts.

El Paso County, Colorado[1]

El Paso County (EPC) is an example of a community that has instituted practices and policies to promote the placement of children who enter foster care with "regular" foster families.[2] The philosophy of EPC, an Annie E. Casey Family-to-Family grant recipient, is that caseworkers should make all efforts to place a child in the child's community of origin and in the "first, best, and only" placement. EPC does not use emer-

gency shelters and does not designate beds in institutional facilities as
emergency resources. Children are placed in residential treatment
facilities or in group care only when they have very specific treatment
needs that cannot be met by a kin caregiver or a foster family.

Why EPC changed its placement practices. EPC undertook a
serious examination of its placement practices for children entering
foster care when it began implementing the Temporary Assistance to
Needy Families (TANF) program in 1996. At that time, David Berns,
Director, and Barbara Drake, Deputy Director, of the EPC
Department of Human Services, noted that the populations served by
the county's TANF system and child welfare system overlapped. They
focused on re-engineering both systems to promote programs that
emphasized prevention, as well as intervention services to combat
poverty and other problems that affect child safety and well-being.
Berns and Drake solicited ideas and support from child welfare professionals and community-based organizations who they identified as
the key stakeholders in the county. The county commissioner supported the effort and worked to ensure flexibility in reallocating funding streams to support the re-engineering of the two systems. In
rethinking the structure of both programs simultaneously, the county
determined that "TANF must be a primary prevention program for
child welfare and child welfare must become an anti-poverty program"
(Berns & Drake, 1999, p. 28).

To integrate the TANF and child welfare programs, the county
developed a common vision and mission for the two programs. The
mission statement became: "To strengthen families, assure safety, promote self-sufficiency, eliminate poverty, and improve the quality of
life in our community" (EPC Department of Human Services, 2004).
EPC also developed a set of guiding principles as the central tenets for
service provision through the TANF and child welfare systems. These
guiding principles state that a system of care must:

- be family-driven;
- have programs that are effectively integrated;
- be strengths-based, with services delivered in the least intrusive way possible;
- have services that are accessible, accountable, and comprehensive;
- meet the individualized needs of families;
- be coordinated across systems;
- emphasize prevention and early intervention;
- provide seamless transitions between programs as families grow and develop;
- protect the rights of families;
- evaluate outcomes of all services; and
- have services delivered in a culturally respectful way by competent staff (Berns et al., 1999).

EPC's child welfare system is fully privatized. EPC contracts with nine local child placement agencies (CPAs) to recruit, certify, supervise, and provide support services to foster families. CPAs are responsible for providing casework services to families and to children placed with foster families whom the CPAs have licensed. CPAs provide planning, court intervention, and adoption services, when appropriate. EPC provides oversight for all CPAs and has designated staff to monitor the process and outcomes of these programs. EPC also has focused on maximizing its Medicaid funding and has restructured its managed care contracts with Medicaid providers and with CPAs to ensure maximum coordination on individual cases.

Prior to implementing its new approach, EPC had contracted with residential treatment centers and group homes for the use of emergency shelter beds as placement resources for children entering foster care. The new program design eliminated these beds. EPC had also used emergency foster homes as initial placement resources and had paid these families a premium rate for the temporary care of children of up to 30 days. EPC's experience, however, was that emergency care with foster families was not temporary, and in many cases, foster families were paid the premium rate for the extended periods of time that children were in their care, often for months.

In the new design, every foster family home is considered an emergency placement, and every family is paid under a new rate system. All foster parents receive an enhanced rate for the first month a child is in their care. The enhanced rate recognizes that the first month of a child's care is generally the most labor intensive for foster families, who must obtain a range of medical and mental health assessments and services for the child, enroll the child in school, and attend court hearings. EPC also implemented a reimbursement system based on "difficulty of care" criteria. With the implementation of the new program and the elimination of shelter beds in institutions, EPC has reduced the institutionalization of children by 40%.

A number of researchers and child welfare professionals have evaluated EPC's programs. Several reports have highlighted the county's innovative thinking and programming, particularly its efforts to address poverty issues and child welfare issues simultaneously. Most recently, the Center for Law and Social Policy (Hutson, 2003) and the Urban Institute (Capizzano, Koralek, Botsko, & Bess, 2001) published reports that document the successful changes the county has made in both the TANF and child welfare systems.

Services for children and families. EPC's child population is approximately 145,000, and approximately 650 children are in foster care in any given month. The county currently has approximately 250 family foster homes and 80 kinship homes, four residential treatment programs, and seven other congregate care facilities. County administrators reported that it was difficult to accurately state the time that children spend in foster care because time in care is highly dependent on the individual needs and circumstances of each child, and the county's concurrent planning and permanency efforts affect the number of days a child is in care. Statistics from EPC indicate, however, that children remain in foster care, on average, for five to six months. Data also indicate that 75% to 80% of children return home within 12 to 18 months and that 10% to 15% of children remain in care longer than 18 months. As a comparison, national data indicate that 68% of children are reunified within 12 months of entry into foster care (DHHS, 2003).[3]

Because of its commitment to early intervention and prevention programs for families, EPC has focused its resources on in-home services for children and families. When children must be removed from their parents' custody, EPC considers care with kin before placing a child with an unrelated foster family. If a child must be placed in out-of-home care with an unrelated foster family, a co-located placement team comprised of county workers and CPA caseworkers work together to identify the best placement for the child.

EPC's emergency care services have four components: intensive home-based services, kinship homes, community-based foster homes, and a subsidized permanent custody with relatives program.

- **Intensive home-based services.** EPC provides intensive in-home services to families to avoid the removal of children from families, whenever possible. These services may include: mental health and substance abuse treatment, crisis intervention, emergency financial assistance, and concentrated assistance in skills development and improvement, such as parenting instruction, stress reduction, problem solving, household budget management, and the use of community resources (Hutson, 2003). A local network of service providers delivers these services through a managed care contract. Contractors must report on specific indicators, and performance on the indicators is tied to incentive payments (Hutson, 2003).

- **Kinship homes.** The EPC Department of Human Services certifies and supervises kinship homes, which are the only placement resources that are administered directly by the county (Colorado Department of Human Services [CDHS], 2002). When child protection caseworkers identify relative caregivers for children, they conduct a background check within 24 hours. They encourage relative caregivers who participate in the TANF program to become licensed foster families and receive the regular foster care rate. EPC works to identify and license maternal and paternal relatives, provides financial support and services for families who care for their relative children, and involves relatives in decisionmaking through family team meetings (CDHS, 2002). Despite these efforts, EPC reports a one-third disruption rate of kinship placements because of kin caregivers' difficulties with the children's birthparents or the children in their care (personal communication, key informant from Colorado, February 5, 2004).

- **Community-based foster homes.** EPC's community-based foster care model is implemented, as noted earlier, through contracts with nine local CPAs that certify, supervise, and provide support services to foster families through performance-based managed care contracts. Under CDHS oversight, CPAs place children with appropriate foster families (or in appropriate residential or group care facilities), provide case management services, and comply with court procedures. They are expected to provide services to meet children's needs and to achieve permanence as soon as is safely possible. CPAs' recruitment and retention of foster families is strengthened by the use of the Family-to-Family program model. A Medicaid managed care contract provides additional services. A therapist conducts a full assessment of each child's mental health needs within a week of the child's placement into care, and mental health staff serve as care coordinators throughout the duration of the child's time in care (CDHS, 2002).

- **Subsidized permanent custody with relatives program.** Subsidies are available through EPC for relatives who assume permanent custody of a child in their care, meet TANF eligibility requirements, have been certified as foster parents, and have received a difficulty of care reimbursement for a child in foster care (CDHS, 2002). EPC must determine that the subsidized permanent custody arrangement is the best permanent arrangement for the child, and the family must not have any safety issues that would require an ongoing child welfare case (CDHS, 2002). Under the program, the relative caregiver is eligible to receive a TANF benefit up to the level of the difficulty of care payment. The caseworker reviews the relative caregiver's financial needs yearly, and the caregiver has access to social work services through TANF, if such services are needed (CDHS, 2002).

Successes and challenges. Many aspects of EPC's effort have been successful. Privatization has facilitated the coordination of child welfare services through the use of performance-based contracts. Politicians and voters have viewed privatization favorably because it has limited the role of government, an important political issue in this county. In spite of scarce funding resources, EPC has developed sustainable programs through the flexible and creative use of federal and state funding. EPC, for example, has used the savings realized from reducing its reliance on institutional care to increase the reimbursement rates for foster families and to reduce caseloads. By using savings from institutional care reductions to pay for additional casework staff, caseloads are currently 12 to 15 children per caseworker, down from 30 children per caseworker. The county reports positive outcomes in three specific areas:

1. **Heightened efficiency**—EPC has increased efficiency by assigning one caseworker to each family. Multiple caseworkers are not involved with the same family. Staff view privatizing casework functions as making this efficiency possible.

2. **Maximization of federal funds**—EPC has used TANF money for preventive services to support and strengthen families and has created new services for families within the TANF program. It also has used Medicaid funding to provide services for children and families through community providers.

3. **Improved outcomes**—EPC has successfully reduced the number of children in out-of-home care and the number of children in institutional care. It also has assisted a larger number of families to transition from poverty to self-sufficiency.

EPC cites its success in working with CPAs to recruit, maintain, and support foster families for children in care. The collaboration between county and private agency staff has been a critical part of the effort's success. A Colorado State Review Team Evaluation (Colorado Department of Human Services, 2002) noted that

> county staff and private service workers work closely together in the office, often as members of the same team. This teaming strengthens connections between programs, increases awareness of the availability of a wider range of services, and facilitates sharing a common vision and goals.

The evaluation also noted that "David Berns has been successful in providing dynamic and innovative leadership that has resulted in a resource-rich human service environment." In addition, EPC has cited the CPAs' diversity as a factor in EPC's success. Each agency has its own niche in terms of the children and the families that it serves, and CPAs consequently complement one another rather than competing to provide services for children and families.

EPC also has faced challenges. The administration of the contracts with the nine CPAs has posed challenges because each agency has its own casework philosophy and culture, and each desires to "call the shots" in terms of the services that the agency provides. In many cases, CPAs have had to expand service into areas that are not familiar to them to meet the needs of children and families. CPAs also have different quality management practices that have posed difficulties in the reporting of standardized data. CPAs have faced challenges in recruiting foster families, a challenge encountered in most communities across the United States. Finally, EPC staff stated that accessing federal and state funding for the program is a constant challenge, despite the flexibility and creativity that it has brought to the effort.

Marion County, Indiana[4]

Marion County (MC), Indiana, is a community that has focused on reducing its reliance on emergency shelter care and building a family-based model of care for children entering foster care. MC, however, has struggled to overcome the prevailing wisdom in the community that places a high value on shelters as a placement resource for children entering foster care. Although the juvenile court system and the county's Office of Family and Children have worked to develop and implement a family-based care model, they have encountered strong community support for the continuation of a large emergency shelter for children, the Children's Guardian Home, that has operated in MC since 1898. MC has fought what might be termed as an "uphill battle," but it has, in many ways, been successful in its efforts to redesign its placement practice and modify the role of a beloved community institution.

Why MC changed its placement practices. In the late 1990s, Judge James W. Payne, a juvenile court judge with 19 years of experience on the bench, sparked efforts to change placement practices in MC. Recognizing that removing children from their families and placing them in a large emergency shelter was not in children's best interests, he began to advocate for two significant changes in current practice: (1) developing and integrating an assessment component into the intake process for each child entering foster care and (2) making greater efforts to place children with kin or unrelated foster families before resorting to shelter care placements. The county, during this same time period, was becoming aware of the growing costs associated with shelter care, costs that had increased 31% a year over the preceding five years and had grown from $7 million to $32 million annually. Judge Payne's leadership in making significant changes in the county's placement practice and the county's concerns about the rising cost of shelter care prompted a re-engineering of MC's placement practices.

As a first step in this effort, the county held a series of community meetings. It had strong support from the mayor's office, the TANF program, the courts, and community mental health centers to develop a new program and service structure.[5] Working together, the various agencies developed a plan to create a stand-alone assessment center to be available 24 hours a day, seven days a week that would provide services to facilitate the placement of children entering foster care and would provide overnight care, if needed. The county issued a request for proposals, and it selected Indiana Behavioral Choices, a nonprofit organization developed by four major mental health organizations, as the entity to develop and operate the assessment center.

The new program, Youth Emergency Services (YES), involves the co-location and coordination of county child protective workers and YES staff, who work together to determine whether a child's removal from his or her family is necessary, and if so, the appropriate placement for the child. YES encountered challenges initially in implementing this aspect of the program because the county's child protective services (CPS) had limited hours of operation, from 8:00 A.M. to 4:30 P.M., Monday through Friday. During these times, CPS determined whether to remove children from their families and place them in care. Outside these hours, the police made these decisions and routinely brought children to the Children's Guardian Home, the large community shelter. With the implementation of YES, CPS needed to be available 24 hours a day, seven day a week. The county successfully engaged in negotiations with the state to develop and fund two additional shifts of CPS staff and offer full-time, around-the-clock CPS coverage. This step was critical to the success of YES.

As part of its redesign of placement practices, MC developed policies and practices to limit shelter care to only those situations in which children had "absolutely no other placement options." At the same time, however, that MC was developing these policies and practices, the Children's Guardian Home undertook a multimillion-dollar campaign to rebuild and expand its aging campus. The Children's Guardian Home viewed the county's actions as hostile to its efforts and claimed that YES would "shut them down." The resulting tension between the Children's Guardian Home and the county created a dilemma for many politicians and community members who supported both YES and the expansion of the well-regarded emergency shelter. In the end, a compromise among the various parties was reached, and the Children's Guardian Home agreed to limit its expansion to half the number of beds originally planned. A relationship among the Guardian Home, YES, and CPA has evolved slowly over time, and the county reports that these entities now work together in a collaborative and cooperative manner.

The county readily concedes that the start-up of YES created "lots of issues" and confusion for caseworkers. MC invested significant time and resources in defining program roles and conducted many meetings with community stakeholders to overcome the range of challenges it encountered. One county administrator, for example, described holding a meeting with YES program staff at 3:00 A.M. to work with them on the challenges that they were encountering. The ability of county administrators and caseworkers to articulate their needs and clarify the roles of the many entities involved with the program, however, has led to effective working relationships. MC considers YES a great success.

Services for children and families. All placement decisions and family assessments are the joint responsibility of YES and CPS. Whenever possible, children who must enter foster care are placed with kin or unrelated foster families. The Children's Guardian Home is used as a last-resort resource for children for whom no other placement resource is available.

In 2003, YES served 3,079 children. More than half of these children were children of color (48% were African American, 37% were white, 6% were biracial, and 9% were classified as of unknown ethnicity). Consistent with previous data reflecting that children entering foster care were young, more than half of the children were younger than 7. With regard to the dispositions for these children, workers reunified more than half of children served through YES with their families or placed them with relatives, placed 12% with foster families, and referred 25% to the Children's Guardian Home (YES, 2003).

The Children's Guardian Home reports a decline in the number of children that it serves, but it also reports that children spend longer periods of time at the facility. In 2003, 2,198 children were placed at the facility, a 4.2% decrease from 2002. Of the children served during 2003, half were African American, 41% were white, 3% were biracial, and 4% were Hispanic. The average daily census was 49 children. Older children (ages 6 and older) stayed an average of nine days, and younger children (ages 5 and younger) remained an average of six days. Approximately 86% of children initially placed at the Children's Guardian Home leave for family-based placements: 39% are reunited with their birthfamilies, 30% are placed with foster families, and 16.6% are placed with relatives (MC Children's Guardian Home, 2003).

The county's emergency care services have two components: YES and the Children's Guardian Home.

YES.[6] Under its fee-for-service contract with the MC Office of Family and Children, YES provides services to families whose children are at risk of coming into foster care and families already involved with the child welfare system. YES is designed to "intervene at the point of a crisis to keep families together" or, if the child's safety is in question, to assist in the child's removal from the family and the child's foster care placement. YES services include: crisis intervention, assessment, referrals, and assistance to CPS in finding homelike placements for children entering foster care. YES conducts individual assessments of children, conducts relative placement assessments, and develops safety plans with families. A YES crisis counselor conducts an age-appropriate assessment on each child, either at the YES center or at the family's home. YES bachelor's-level crisis counselors receive three to four weeks of specialized training in assessing children and families in crisis. They conduct assessments under the supervision of master's-level clinicians.

One-quarter to one-third of the requests that YES receives involve assessments of kin as placement resources for children in need of foster care services. If YES determines that a relative's home is a safe and appropriate placement for a child, YES staff may work with the relative to develop a safety plan to ensure that family members who may pose a danger to the child do not have access to the child. YES crisis counselors also may facilitate safety plans with parents so that children do not need to be removed from their families.

The success of YES rests in its team approach to working with children and families and the collaboration among the MC Office of Family and Children case managers, law enforcement officers, emergency dispatch personnel, foster care case managers, and foster parents. YES staff often accompany Office of Family and Children case managers to meetings with families. YES often is in contact with county case managers by cell phone, a practice that allows for prompt planning and services for children. Collaboration with law enforcement is particularly important because, in many cases, it is law enforcement that provides the first information about a family crisis. Information that law enforcement officers gather often assists YES and CPS staff in locating kin as caregivers for children. When an assessment of kin is requested, YES works with the Juvenile Justice Center to obtain necessary information, including criminal record checks.

YES staff has responsibility for placing children with foster families after 4:30 P.M. on weekdays and on weekends. YES crisis counselors work closely with foster families and communicate information about children's functioning and needs. YES staff also work with the Children's Guardian Home when children have no kinship or foster family options. In these situations, YES coordinates needed services for children.

The Children's Guardian Home.[7] Supported by county funds for its operating expenses and by funds from its private foundation for facility maintenance, the Children's Guardian Home provides 24-hour emergency shelter services. Its census fluctuates depending on the time of year, the general economic climate, and the extent of unemployment in the community.

Organized "like a large school," the Children's Guardian Home is licensed to care for 80 children from infancy to 18 years old. A nursery serves both male and female children who are younger than 5 years. The nursery has an "infants room" and a "toddlers room" for sleeping and a separate day care area. Although initially licensed to serve only 8 infants or toddlers, the facility recently expanded its capacity to 18 infants and toddlers to meet the demand for shelter care for younger children. Children older than 5 live in separate dormitories, three dormitories for girls and two dormitories for boys. Each dormitory has five bedrooms that accommodate two or three children each. Consistent with state mandates, staffing ratios are 12:1 during the day and 20:1 at night for children 5 years of age and older and 6:1 for younger children during the day and night.

Social workers at the Children's Guardian Home provide crisis intervention services and case management services for children at the facility. A psychiatric social worker, under contract with a local mental health agency, is onsite 2.5 days each week. A certified nursing specialist assesses the psychiatric needs of children. A licensed pediatrician, dentist, and nurse practitioner (who is onsite 40 hours each week) oversee medical and dental care. A school counselor coordinates educational services and enrolls children in school, if necessary. Federally funded tutoring is available onsite. A recreation coordinator oversees a program of activities for the children.

On a daily basis, YES staff confer with facility staff about children's case plans and service needs. YES staff provide facility staff with behavioral observations and medical information pertinent to the care of children. YES staff transport children to the Children's Guardian Home when children are placed at the facility and to and from the facility when YES provides assessment or case planning.

Successes and Challenges. Juvenile court leadership was a critical factor in the county's implementation of changes in its placement practices. MC admittedly has many challenges to overcome, but several factors have promoted success in specific areas. The biggest strength is the communication and collaboration among the various agencies that serve children and families. After three years of concentrated work, YES staff, Children's Guardian Home staff, CPS workers, law enforcement, and the juvenile courts have effective relationships. Stakeholders describe the collaboration as "amazing" and as "central to making the system work" and report that caseworkers see one other as "true partners." The physical proximity of caseworkers to one another is a key factor in promoting staff collaboration. YES staff and CPS caseworkers work in adjacent offices, which supports communication and collaboration. As one county stakeholder stated, "You have to know the people you're working with to trust them; personal relationships and mutual respect between workers benefit both staff and the children and families we serve." Monthly meetings of all key players also facilitate communication and mutual problem solving.

Flexibility is another strength of the programs. As a private nonprofit group, YES has flexibility in staffing and resources, which allows it to adapt its services as necessary to meet the changing needs of children and families. YES has had a low staff turnover rate because it is able to pay staff well and support staff with training, supervision, and resources.

MC, nonetheless, faces some significant challenges. MC and Indiana are struggling with a "foster care crisis" precipitated by budget shortfalls for child welfare services and an increase in the number of children coming into foster care as a result of parental drug use. County caseworkers currently average caseloads of 50 children (CWLA standards recommend 15 children per caseworker; CWLA, 1995, Standard 3.48), and the state is not able to fill vacant positions because of budgetary constraints. These conditions have affected the county's ability to work as effectively as possible with YES.

Professionals in MC also express views that the county's foster family recruiting and licensing program is "notably bad." Currently, the Indiana Foster Parent Association holds the contract with the state to recruit foster families statewide. In that structure, each county is to develop its own foster family recruitment plan. MC has had considerable confusion about who is responsible for developing the plan, and professionals report that no recruiting plan is currently in place. In an effort to rectify this situation, MC has formed a taskforce to develop a plan to improve its foster family recruitment efforts. With regard to licensing foster families, county professionals describe the process as "frustrating" and "overly bureaucratic" and report that it can take months to complete the licensing of foster families. The challenges posed by the current recruiting and licensing processes are further exacerbated by inadequate financial support and services for foster families. These issues have limited the number of foster families available to meet children's placement needs, and, as a consequence, MC has continued to rely heavily on the Children's Guardian Home despite diligent efforts to change this practice.

Contra Costa County, California[8]

Contra Costa County (CCC) is the site of three receiving centers. Having centralized its placement resources, the county relies on receiving centers as the point of entry for all children and youth entering foster care.

Why CCC changed its placement practices. As one of the first counties in California to develop a receiving center system, CCC began its program in September 1997. CCC previously used an emergency shelter and emergency foster homes located throughout the county. Danna Fabella, Director of the Child and Family Services Bureau, and her colleagues developed the receiving center system in an effort to better coordinate the placement of children into foster care and to meet the needs of children and their caregivers. They envisioned a continuum of care so that children could be placed appropriately, preferably with kin, and they designed receiving centers to achieve that vision. Based on data collected from the county's assessments of who used child welfare services, when, and where, they determined where receiving centers should be located, and they structured the services to meet the needs that children, families, and caseworkers identified.

As the hub for emergency placement activities, three receiving centers operate through contracts with three different nonprofit groups based in the communities of Richmond, Concord, and Antioch. The receiving centers are supported solely with county funds, because they are not considered a placement or shelter facility that would permit the use of state or federal child welfare funding.[9] The center's operations are structured to maximize limited funding and to provide services as needed.

The three receiving centers are open 24 hours a day, seven days a week. The core business hours, based on the county's utilization data, are between 9:00 A.M. and 8:00 P.M., and during these hours, staff provide onsite services for children, families, and caseworkers. If assistance is needed outside these hours, a caseworker pages receiving center staff and they meet caseworkers and families at the center.

Emergency foster homes are available as placement resources for children as part of the overall emergency care system for the county. These homes are county licensed and serve as temporary placements for children after children have been seen at a receiving center. Foster family agencies, which are privately operated and licensed foster care agencies in the county, also provide emergency placement services for children who need higher levels of care than county emergency foster families can provide. The county also maintains two group homes for children which caseworkers use when children have experienced multiple disruptions when placed with foster families and when children prefer group care.

As of June 2004, CCC had approximately 270 children in its emergency care system. Most children were younger than age 6 (41%). One-fifth (19%) were between the ages of 7 and 11 years, and 37% were between the ages of 12 and 18. Most of these children entered care as part of a sibling group. Approximately three-quarters of children in CCC enter care as a result of neglect. Many parents suffer from substance abuse problems.

Although CCC attempts to limit children's stays in emergency foster homes to 30 days, California child welfare statutes permit stays of up to 90 days. About one-third of the children placed with emergency foster families remain with those families for more than 90 days. Typically, these are children who will be freed for adoption, and efforts are under way to identify an adoptive family for them, or they are children with behavioral problems who require a therapeutic environment. The county's specialized Placement Resource Team, composed of licensing staff, adoption caseworkers, and resources staff, arrange longer-term care for children with behavioral problems and other special needs when children's caseworkers are unable to locate appropriate placements for them within 90 days.

Services provided to children and families. In CCC, receiving centers and emergency family foster care provide emergency care services. As noted, receiving centers facilitate the transition of children into foster care by providing children with food, clothes, and a place to nap and, if necessary, bathe, while social workers make arrangements for the placement of the child. A brief screening identifies any immediate medical or mental health needs that the child may have and documents the physical condition of the child, including any evidence of physical abuse. Children may not remain at receiving centers for longer than 23 hours and 59 minutes. During this time period, county social workers assess placement resources for children, first considering kin. When care with kin is not possible, they place children with unrelated foster families or with emergency foster families until they can make longer-term care arrangements. Receiving centers must comply with the health and safety standards for child care centers. A maximum of 12 children may be present at the receiving center at any point in time. The staffing ratio is one staff member for six children. Additional staff are on call if needed.

Emergency family foster homes are licensed to care for children on a temporary basis. Emergency foster parents receive special training and, by contract, are paid a special rate for emergency beds in their homes ($100 a month per bed) regardless of whether a child is placed with the family. Typically, emergency family foster homes are filled to capacity.

Specialized county staff support emergency foster families. A foster parent liaison assists foster families with problems that arise. Emergency Shelter Care (ESC) workers arrange for respite and other services that foster families need. ESC workers also monitor emergency foster family homes to assess their appropriateness as placements. Finally, CCC offers emergency foster families opportunities to participate in a support group in which they can be resources for one another.

Successes and challenges. CCC views receiving centers as highly valuable because they allow caseworkers time to evaluate a child's needs and assess relatives and others as appropriate placement resources for children, and they provide children with a safe and caring environment while caseworkers are making placement decisions. CCC has found that the retention rate for emergency foster families has increased with the use of receiving centers. Emergency foster families report that they find it easier to provide children with the care they need when children arrive clean, fed, and screened for medical issues and lice.

CCC reports success in both recruiting and retaining emergency foster families. The county focuses on recruiting new families on an ongoing basis and does not view recruitment as a "one-time event." Two recruiters and a public information officer conduct monthly recruitment team meetings with child welfare staff and foster parents and continuously develop and implement new recruitment strategies and campaigns. CCC also offers incentives to current foster families who recruit new foster families.

The county's biggest challenge rests in securing the funding needed for receiving centers. Because the state does not provide funding for receiving centers, the county must use its own funds to fully support this program. County funding for the centers, however, has declined by approximately 10% in each of the last two years. Staff have serious concerns that the receiving centers will have to be closed if they cannot secure adequate funding.

The county also faces challenges related to large caseloads and delays in placing children in emergency care placements into longer-term care arrangements in a timely way. High caseloads often impede efforts to move children from emergency settings into longer-term care arrangements, and children's stays in "temporary" care arrangements, as a result, are often longer than the 30 days the county has set as a goal. CCC currently is working to decrease caseload sizes and move children into longer-term care arrangements more quickly, but funding constraints may mean that these goals will not be immediately attainable.

CHAPTER 5

A Synthesis of Current Practice in Emergency Care Services

I t is common practice across the United States to place children and youth in emergency care settings when they enter foster care. In some cases, agencies use emergency care when caseworkers cannot make alternative care arrangements in children's extended families or with unrelated foster families. In other cases, however, agencies routinely use emergency care as children's points of entry into the foster care system. This study focused on the three primary types of emergency care for children and youth who enter foster care: emergency shelters, emergency family foster care, and receiving centers. It examined how child welfare systems currently use emergency care services and how three communities have worked to change their placement practices. It identified a number of policy and practice factors that often prolong communities' reliance on emergency care despite efforts to implement family-based care.

Research has not focused on emergency care services, and there is little evidence-based practice in this area. Currently, no empirical evidence documents the outcomes associated with children's placements in emergency shelter care, emergency family foster care, or receiving centers. It is, in fact, not clear to what extent agencies use these types of emergency care because neither the federal database (AFCARS) nor most state data systems track children's placements in these settings or the services they receive when in these care arrangements.

The researchers designed this qualitative study to achieve a better understanding of professionals' views of the use of emergency care services throughout the country and the services' effect on children and youth and to learn more about emergency care directly from communities that have altered or attempted to alter their placement practices. The paucity of information about the use of emergency shelters, emergency family foster care, and receiving centers emphasized the importance of gathering information from a cross-section of child welfare professionals—researchers, consultants, county administrators, and leaders of community agencies—about current practices and the issues that warrant critical assessment. This information was enhanced by case studies of three communities that have grappled directly with the use of different emergency care approaches.

The extent to which communities use emergency care services and the types of emergency care that they use are affected by a range of factors: the community's perspective on the appropriateness and need for emergency care services, the caseloads of social workers who make placement decisions, the availability of family-based placement resources, the political will to examine and change placement practices, and the availability of funding. Although this study identified several communities that have reconsidered their reliance on emergency care, it was surprising to find that these communities were in a minority. The general absence of attention to emergency care suggests that emergency care services need to be examined more critically at both the national and state levels. Concerns about the use of emergency care fall squarely within the focus of the Adoption and Safe Families Act of 1997 with its emphasis on the safety, permanence, and the well-being of children, and they are highly relevant to federal evaluation efforts through the Child and Family Services Reviews.

This study found marked discrepancies between what is considered quality emergency care practice and what constitutes current emergency care practice. A clear example is found in the variance between states' and counties' time limits on children's stays in emergency care, as stated in jurisdictions' legislation or policy, and children's actual lengths of stay in emergency care settings. Routinely, staff reported that children remain in emergency care for time periods that exceed the designated time limits. Child welfare professionals reported that certain children spend particularly long periods of time in emergency care settings: older children, children of color, and children with emotional and behavioral problems.

Multiple reasons have been advanced for this outcome. Consistently, child care professionals reported that a shortage of placement resources, including both foster families and residential treatment beds, made it difficult to move children from emergency care settings. They, however, consistently expressed concerns that caseworkers do not make timely efforts to meet children's ongoing placement needs when children are placed in emergency settings, often beginning the planning process just as the time limit for emergency care is expiring. Although they acknowledged that this practice may be the result of a shortage of caseworkers and unreasonable caseloads, they noted that this practice results in many children remaining in emergency care for excessive periods of time with poor outcomes in terms of their safety, well-being, and permanence.

In connection with children's well-being, key informants also consistently reported that many children remain in emergency care, particularly emergency shelters, without receiving necessary medical and mental health services or being enrolled in school in a timely way or at all. They described coordination among the health care, education, and child welfare systems as poor. A number of professionals emphasized that despite children's eligibility for Medicaid and services covered by state and federal child welfare funding, many children in emergency care settings do not receive the health or mental health services they need immediately. Of equal concern was the failure of emergency care providers to ensure that children are enrolled in and attend school. Despite educational entitlements for children in the federal McKinney-Vento Homeless Assistance Act, for example, many children in emergency shelters are not allowed to remain in their schools of origin and are not enrolled in new schools.

Professionals also stated concerns about the effect of long stays in emergency shelters on children's health and well-being. They consistently described shelter care as less safe than family foster care, failing to give individualized attention to children, and not effective at stabilizing children after the trauma of being removed from their families. Their perceptions of emergency care directly contradicted the literature that has promoted emergency shelters as safe and therapeutic environments. In general, the professionals who were interviewed concluded that emergency shelters often were detrimental environments for infants, toddlers, and latency-age children because they fail to meet children's developmental and emotional needs.

Based on the interviews with professionals and the case studies, the researchers found that children and youth are placed in shelter care for two major reasons: a shortage of foster families and the convenience of caseworkers and law enforcement officials. Agencies use emergency shelters more in urban areas and in large counties for these reasons. Urban communities and large counties tend to have larger caseloads and fewer family-based resources, and they have simply accepted shelters as a necessary response to the placement needs of children.

The majority of child welfare professionals viewed family foster care as the best type of emergency care service because it can serve children of all ages, it meets the needs of the majority of children who enter foster care, and it is more economical than other placement options. They also believed that family foster care can more successfully stabilize children after they have been removed from their families. Key informants stated that foster families provide children with more individualized attention and, as a result, are better at obtaining needed assessments and services for children in their care.

Emergency family foster care as a service varies significantly across the states and counties. Some states and counties, for example, place children with emergency foster families under very limited circumstances and then move children within two to three days to longer-care arrangements. Other states and counties certify all foster families as emergency care providers for children entering care and consistently place children with emergency foster families. Irrespective of these differences, virtually all communities appear to struggle to maintain an adequate number of foster families to meet the placement needs of children entering foster care. In response to this conundrum, some communities have privatized their foster care systems, whereas other communities have engaged in broad public education and community efforts to recruit and retain families. The professionals interviewed in this study stated that relationship building, mentoring, and support for foster families are the essential components of any program. They also identified foster parent associations as strong supports for foster families and as effective partners who can ease burdens on county child welfare systems while providing support for families. Although there was consensus on effective recruitment and retention approaches, there also was agreement that resources to develop viable programs are lacking. The lack of resources and the challenges associated with foster family recruitment have led to perceptions that residential care is "easier to do" than family foster care, despite the fact that residential care is more expensive and offers less individualized attention to the needs of children.

The use of receiving centers to facilitate placement decisions is an interesting new model that should be closely monitored and evaluated. Because these centers are not intended as placements for children entering care, staff have no expectation that children will be housed in these facilities, and the focus, instead, is on the child's immediate needs. Receiving centers attempt to meet the needs of children by offering placement and assessment services 24 hours a day, seven days a week, and by providing caseworkers with time and information to make the best placements for children. Key informants familiar with receiving centers reported that they can help prevent placement failures and strengthen the ability of caseworkers to locate the "right," as opposed to simply the "first available" placement for a child. Some also stated that receiving centers can help stabilize children and can support foster families by providing them with more complete information about a child. Some professionals, however, expressed reservations about receiving centers. They questioned the validity of assessments conducted in an "artificial setting" and expressed concern that receiving centers simply are yet another unnecessary stop for children entering care.

The communities that were the subject of the case studies—EPC, MC, and CCC–provided specific information regarding efforts to change emergency care practices and expanded the understanding of the factors that facilitate communities' efforts to implement family-based placement practices and the obstacles to these efforts. The case studies suggest that changes in placement practice are complex and the factors that promote or hinder such changes may vary from one community to another. The case studies highlighted three communities with strong family-based care values that have made significant changes as the result of strong leadership and political will. These communities developed a range of creative strategies, including innovative funding approaches and strong partnerships among multiple agencies in their communities. Although each community has encountered hurdles that they have not always been able to fully surmount, their efforts to make significant changes in emergency care practice provide strong examples for other communities to consider.

Chapter 6

Guiding Principles and Recommendations for Quality Placements and Services for Children in Foster Care

Guiding Principles for Quality Placements for Children in Foster Care

Based on the information gained from the key informant interviews and the experiences of the communities on which the case studies focused, it is possible to identify guiding principles that can provide a foundation for changing placement practice and promoting the placement of children with "regular" foster families when children enter care. The following principles provide a framework for assessing the use of emergency care services for children entering the foster care system:

1. Children and youth are best served in times of crisis by supportive and caring relatives or by foster families who are committed to caring for children and youth for as long as they need care.

2. Foster families must receive support and resources to best help children and their families in times of crisis.

3. Child welfare professionals must receive adequate support, training, and resources to meet the needs of the children and families they serve.

4. To ensure quality care and services for children and their families, child welfare systems must engage in rigorous quality assurance

and evaluation efforts to determine whether their programs meet the needs of the children and families they serve.

Recommendations for Quality Placements for Children in Foster Care

Children in foster care who cannot be placed with kin are best served when they live with unrelated foster families who can meet their individual needs. Of utmost importance are effective programs that recruit, screen, train, and provide ongoing support for foster families, programs that often involve partnerships with foster parent associations and a range of community providers. The findings of this study suggest that communities that are interested in implementing a family-based, nontemporary placement system for children and youth need to take a number of steps. The following recommendations, which are consistent with the work of the Annie E. Casey Foundation's Family-to-Family Initiative and with CWLA standards of best practice, promote family foster care as the most effective approach to meeting the placement needs of children and youth entering foster care.

To provide children and youth with safe, nurturing, and thoughtful care arrangements when they enter foster care, state and county child welfare agencies should:

Recommendation #1. Actively recruit, train, and support foster families as resources for all children entering foster care. Some counties have recognized that foster families are the foundation on which quality foster care is based. Some counties have eliminated the use of emergency shelters and created systems that result in the immediate placement of children with foster families, including EPC, which was highlighted in this study, Lucas County, Ohio, and Cuyahoga County, Ohio, which have made significant changes in their placement practices.[1] In these communities, foster families are matched with children and efforts are made to support these foster families as children's only foster families while they are in care.

To effectively recruit foster families, states and counties should:

- develop and implement comprehensive foster family recruitment strategies that raise public awareness about the need for foster parents;

- recruit foster families as specific placement resources for groups of children often considered hard to place, such as sibling groups, children with emotional disturbances, children with behavior problems, and medically fragile children, and train and support foster families to serve as therapeutic foster families for children with emotional or behavioral issues; and

- partner with a wide variety of community organizations, such as churches, community groups, social service agencies, schools, hospitals, and mental health clinics, to facilitate the recruitment and support of foster families in the community.

To effectively license foster families, states and counties should:

- Support foster families throughout the licensing process so that they have realistic expectations about what it means to be a foster family and have access to information and support as they complete the process and become licensed.

- Create efficient licensing procedures that encourage new foster families to become licensed.

To effectively train and support foster families, states and counties should:

- Provide foster families with training in child development, the effects of child trauma, child welfare policy, and the rights of children in foster care to education, health, and mental health services.

- Develop foster parent support services to assist families with children in their care. Examples of essential support services are: a hotline to provide foster parents with information and guidance, foster parent support groups so that seasoned foster families can support newer foster families, and respite services for foster parents on an as-needed basis.
- Support newer foster parents and respite services for foster parents on an as-needed basis.

Recommendation #2. Eliminate or, at minimum, reduce the use of shelter care and promote placement of children with foster families. Research suggests that care by foster families who are committed to caring for children for as long as they need care promotes the health and well-being of children. The key informants interviewed in this study and professionals in El Paso, Marion, and Contra Costa counties agreed that shelter care is not in children's best interests and that foster families who are committed to children on a longer-term basis, when needed, are best able to promote children's safety, well-being, and permanence. With those principles in mind, states and counties should:

- recognize the importance of serving children, both developmentally and emotionally, in a family context;
- eliminate or, at minimum, reduce reliance on emergency shelter care as a placement option for children entering foster care;
- include youth, birthfamilies, relatives, and foster families in decisions regarding the placements for children and youth;
- place sibling groups together and with families, whenever possible; and
- ensure that the number of placement moves for each child is kept at a bare minimum, consistent with the "first placement, best placement, only placement" philosophy.

Recommendation #3. Provide adequate infrastructure, training, and support for caseworkers to ensure they have the skills and resources necessary for assisting children and families in crisis and making the best placement decisions. It is essential that states and counties develop an infrastructure that supports quality casework. Caseloads should conform to the standards CWLA has set forth. Training and supervision should communicate and reinforce the principles of quality placement practice and ensure that caseworkers have the knowledge and skills that they need to assess children and families, assess placement options, and make sound placement decisions. States and counties should:

- maintain caseloads that are consistent with CWLA caseload standards;
- ensure that caseworkers have comprehensive knowledge of child development and the effects of trauma on children, and receive ongoing training on crisis intervention, strengths-based culturally competent practice, and placement decisionmaking;
- ensure that caseworkers understand federal and state mandates regarding the rights of children, birthfamilies, and foster families;
- ensure weekly one-on-one supervision for caseworkers to provide support and assist them with decisionmaking on children's placements and services; and
- ensure that caseworkers have immediate access to information on foster family resources and on services for children, birthfamilies, and foster families.

Recommendation #4. Develop or enhance evaluation systems to monitor outcomes associated with emergency care services. To date, research has not addressed the extent to which different forms of emergency care meet the needs of children for safety, well-being, and permanence or involve families in planning for their children. An in-depth examination of the outcomes for children placed in emergency shelters and emergency family foster care is essential. Evaluations of the effect of receiving centers on outcomes for children also is critical. As the Annie E. Casey Foundation (2004) has stated, "Data are a means to testing assumptions, creating focus, and developing an understanding for why practices and programs work or don't work...without data, success is entirely subjective" (p. 22). Research on and evaluation of emergency care services would clarify the types of programs that provide the best outcomes for children and assist policymakers and program administrators in designing, or redesigning, emergency care practice in the most effective way. To this end, states and counties should:

- review current data sources to determine what information on emergency care services exists, identify information gaps, develop criteria used to assess the quality of placements for children, enhance data collection systems to track specified criteria, and develop and implement evaluation mechanisms that obtain consumer feedback; and

- use data to promote accountability and support decision-making about effective or ineffective programs and practices.

Chapter 7

Conclusion

This qualitative study examined the use of three types of emergency care services—emergency shelters, emergency family foster care, and receiving centers—in states and counties across the United States. Key informants described their experiences with emergency care services, discussed the strengths and weaknesses of different forms of emergency care, and provided their views of programs that have successfully made foster families the primary placement resources for children in foster care. This report's case studies demonstrate how three communities are attempting to restructure emergency care practices. This study documents the need for additional research and evaluations of current programmatic approaches and the need to develop evidence-based practice in emergency care services. There appears to be agreement that shelter care does not promote positive outcomes for children and youth; that emergency foster family care is a better, though not optimal, placement option; and that receiving centers offer an interesting but untested approach to facilitating placement decisionmaking. It is hoped that this study contributes to a better understanding of emergency care services and provides the basis for continuing dialogue on an area of child welfare practice that largely has escaped a critical assessment.

Notes

Chapter 1
The Current Knowledge Base on Emergency Care

1. In some counties, receiving centers are known as assessment centers. In this report, the term *receiving center* is used to refer to both receiving and assessment centers.

Chapter 2
The Method

1. These states are Arizona, California, Connecticut, Iowa, Michigan, New Jersey, North Carolina, Ohio, and Rhode Island.

2. Kathy Barbell, Senior Program Director for Program Operations, Child Welfare League of America, Washington, DC; Judith Goodhand, Senior Fellow, Annie E. Casey Foundation, Washington, DC; Elizabeth Leatherman, Technical Assistant, Annie E. Casey Foundation, Columbus, SC; and Jake Terpstra, Child Welfare Consultant, Grand Rapids, MI.

3. Snowball sampling requires an initial set of informants be located through reasonable means and surveyed. The researchers then ask these informants to identify other informants whom they believe are knowledgeable about the matter at issue (Rossi, Freeman, & Lipsey, 1999).

Chapter 4
Changes in Emergency Care Practice: Three Case Studies

1. The researchers would like to thank David Berns, former Director of the El Paso County Department of Human Services, and Lloyd Malone, Child Welfare Director for El Paso County Department of Human Services, for the valuable information that they provided.

2. In Colorado, child protection programs and public assistance programs are operated by individual counties and supervised by the state.

3. No comparable federal data are available to measure how many children remain in care for longer than 18 months. The federal report *Child Welfare Outcomes 2001: Annual Report* (U.S. Department of Health and Human Services, 2004) measures reunification at 12 months and at 24 months.

4. The researchers would like to thank M. B. Lippold, Project Manager for the Child and Adolescent Placement Project, Marion County Superior Court–Juvenile Division; John Kennedy, Director, Youth Emergency Services Program; Lisa Goldberg-Mitton, Supervisor, Youth Emergency Services Program; and Rosie Butler, Director, Marion County Children's Guardian Home, for the valuable information that they provided.

5. For a detailed summary of meetings and activities related to the development of the Youth Emergency Services (YES) program, please refer to the YES Evolution chart in YES (n.d., pp. 6–8).

6. Program information and statistics were obtained by researchers through an interview with John Kennedy, Director, Youth Emergency Services Program, and from the *Youth Emergency Service Annual Report, Year 6, January 1, 2003–December 31, 2003* (available from the authors).

7. Researchers obtained program information and statistics through an interview with Rosie Butler, Director, Marion County Children's Guardian Home, and from the *Marion County Children's Guardian Home 2003 Annual Statistics* (available from the authors).

8. The researchers would like to thank Danna Fabella, Director, Child and Family Services Bureau, Contra Costa County, for the valuable information that she provided.

9. Contra Costa County unsuccessfully sponsored legislation that would have provided state recognition of and funding for receiving centers. The California state legislature favored the use of shelters and other congregate care facilities and refused to provide state funding for receiving centers.

Chapter 6
Guiding Principles and Recommendations

1. El Paso County, Colorado; Lucas County, Ohio; and Cuyahoga County, Ohio, implemented practice changes as part of the Annie E. Casey Family-to-Family Initiative.

References

American Association of University Women. (1970). *Where do children go?* Wilmington, DE: Author.

Annie E. Casey Foundation. (2004). *Family-to-Family tools for rebuilding foster care: Lessons learned.* Retrieved August 3, 2004, from http://www.aecf.org/initiatives/ familytofamily/tools/lessons.pdf.

Barth, R. (2002). *Institutions vs. foster homes: The empirical base for a century action.* Chapel Hill, NC: University of North Carolina, School of Social Work, Jordan Institute for Families.

Berns, D., & Drake, B. (1999). Combining child welfare and welfare reform at a local level. *Policy & Practice of Public Human Services,* 57(1), 26–34.

Capizzano, J., Koralek, R., Botsko, C., & Bess, R. (2001, October 1). *Recent changes in Colorado welfare and work, child care, and child welfare systems* (Assessing the New Federalism, State Update No. 9). Washington, DC: Urban Institute.

Child Welfare League of America. (1995). *Standards of excellence for family foster care services.* Washington, DC: Author.

Child Welfare League of America. (1999). *Standards of excellence for services for abused and neglected children and their families.* Washington, DC: Author.

Child Welfare League of America. (2004). *Standards of excellence for residential services.* Washington, DC: Author.

Choice, P., Deichert, K., Legry, C., & Austin, M. (2000). *Receiving centers and informal emergency assessment settings in child welfare: Child, family, service, and placement characteristics.* Berkeley, CA: Bay Area Social Services Consortium, Center for

Social Services Research, School of Social Welfare, University of California, Berkeley.

Colorado Department of Human Services. (2002). *El Paso County foster care review report, on-site review completed December 11–13, 2002.* Retrieved July 27, 2004, from http://www.cdhs.state.co.us/cyf/cwelfare/Audit%20information/El%20Paso%20FC%20Final% 20Report.pdf.

De Sá, K. (2003, June 2). Counties turning from use of shelters: Displaced kids being sent to relatives, foster homes. *San Jose Mercury News,* 1A.

DeSena, A., Murphy, R., Douglas-Palumberi, H., Blau, G., Kelly, B., & Horowitz, S. (2003, June 5). *SAFE homes: Is it worth the cost? An evaluation of the Connecticut model of intervention for children who enter out-of-home care.* Retrieved July 31, 2004, from http://www.state.ct.us/dcf/Research_Stats/Safe_Homes/SH_retrospective.pdf.

El Paso County Department of Human Services. (2004). *2003 annual summary.* Retrieved July 27, 2004, from http://dhs.elpasoco.com/humansvc/AnnualSum2003.pdf.

Ensign, J. (2001). The health of shelter-based foster youth. *Public Health Nursing,* 18(1), 19–23.

Festinger, T. (1983). *No one ever asked us...A postscript to foster care.* New York: Columbia University Press.

Gershowitz, M., & MacFarlane, A. (1990). The therapeutic potential of emergency shelters. *Child and Youth Services,* 13(1), 95–103.

Hutson, R. (2003). *A vision for eliminating poverty and family violence: Transforming child welfare and TANF in El Paso County, Colorado.* Washington, DC: Center for Law and Social Policy.

Johnson, K. (2003). Emergency diagnostic shelters: Underrated? *Residential Group Care Quarterly,* 4(1), 6–7.

Jones, M., & Moses, B. (1984). *West Virginia's former foster children: Their experiences in care and their lives as young adults.* New York: Child Welfare League of America.

Kools, S. (1997). Adolescent identity development in foster care. *Family Relations, 46,* 263–271.

Litrownik, A. J., Taussig, H. N., Landsverk, J. A., & Garland, A. F. (1999). Youth entering an emergency shelter care facility: Prior involvement in juvenile justice and mental health systems. *Journal of Social Service Research,* 25(3), 5–19.

Marion County Children's Guardian Home. (2003). *Marion County Children's Guardian Home 2003 annual statistics.* Indianapolis, IN: Author.

McDonald, T., Allen, R., Westerfelt, A., & Piliavin, I. (1996). *Assessing the long-term effects of foster care: A research synthesis.* Washington, DC: Child Welfare League of America.

Needell, B., Webster, D., Cuccaro-Alamin, S., Armijo, M., Lee, S., Lery, B., et al. (2004). *Child welfare services reports for California.* Retrieved August 23, 2004, from http://cssr.berkeley.edu/CWSCMSreports/.

Rittner, B. (1995). Children on the move: Placement patterns in children's protective services. *Families in Society, 76,* 469–477.

Rossi, P., Freeman, H., & Lipsey, M. (1999). *Evaluation: A systematic approach* (6th ed.). Thousand Oaks, CA: Sage.

Terpstra, J. (1988). Making the most of shelter care: Strategies for family and community involvement. In G. Carman & R. Small (Eds.), *Permanence and family support: Changing practice in group child care* (pp. 135-149). Washington, DC: Child Welfare League of America.

Terpstra, J. (2003). Emergency shelters. *Residential Group Care Quarterly, 4*(1), 8–9.

U.S. Department of Health and Human Services. (2003). *Child welfare outcomes 2000: Annual report to Congress.* Retrieved August 30, 2004, from http://www.acf.hhs.gov/programs/cb/publications/cwo00/index.htm.

U.S. Department of Health and Human Services. (2004). *Child welfare outcomes 2001: Annual report.* Retrieved November 3, 2004, from http://www.acf.hhs.gov/programs/cb/publications/cwo01/index.htm.

Youth Emergency Services. (2003). *Youth Emergency Services annual report year six, January 1, 2003–December 31, 2003.* Indianapolis, IN: Author.

Youth Emergency Services. (n.d.). *YES: One year review: 1/1/98–12/31/98.* Retrieved July 30, 2004, from http://www.kidwrap.org/pdf/YES_12.pdf.

About the Authors

Emily Joyce Oakes is a Policy Analyst for Children's Rights, New York City, New York. Ms. Oakes' professional experience includes both direct practice social work and research experience in the areas of domestic violence and child trauma. Prior to joining Children's Rights, she was a program coordinator for a National Child Traumatic Stress Network program site—the Safe Horizon/St. Vincent's Child Trauma Care Initiative in New York City. Her current work at Children's Rights focuses on the use of emergency care for children entering the foster care system, the ethics of transracial adoption, and interdisciplinary barriers to adoption. Ms. Oakes holds a bachelor's degree in psychology from Connecticut College and master's degrees in both social work and public administration from Columbia University.

Madelyn Freundlich is the Policy Director for Children's Rights, New York City, New York. She formerly served as the Executive Director of the Evan B. Donaldson Adoption Institute and as General Counsel for the Child Welfare League of America. She is a social worker and lawyer whose work has focused on child welfare policy and practice for the past decade. She has coauthored a number of books on child welfare law and policy, including *Wrongful Adoption: Law, Policy and Practice; Managed Care: An Agency Guide to Surviving and Thriving; and*

Independent Living Services for Youth in Out-of-Home Care. She also has authored a number of articles that address a wide range of topics, including the effect of welfare reform on foster care and special-needs adoption, the role of race and culture in adoption, the use of Medicaid to finance services for children in foster care, interstate adoption law and practice, genetic testing in adoption evaluations, and confidentiality in child welfare practice. Ms. Freundlich holds master's degrees in social work and public health and holds a JD and LLM.

About Children's Rights, Inc.

Children's Rights, Inc. is a national nonprofit organization based in New York City that addresses the needs of abused and neglected children dependent on child welfare systems for protection and care. Children's Rights partners with advocates, experts, policy analysts, and government officials to develop realistic solutions and, if necessary, uses the power of the courts to make sure the rights of these children are recognized and that reform takes place. The Policy Department at Children's Rights, established in 2000, has engaged in a number of initiatives both independently and in collaboration with leading child welfare agencies across the country. The Policy Department conducts independent research focusing on child welfare issues such as permanence, foster care, juvenile justice, and adoption.